"GO FOR BROKE"

"GO FOR BROKE"

JAPANESE AMERICANS- IN WORLD WAR II

BY TOM McGOWEN

A First Book
Franklin Watts
New York / Chicago / London / Toronto / Sydney

For Blake

Cover art by Jane Sterrett

Photographs copyright ©: UPI/Bettmann: pp. 2, 11, 12, 14, 16, 22, 32, 34; Veterans of Foreign Wars of the United States: pp. 8 (National Archives), 55 (Minnesota Historical Society); Library of Congress: p. 15; National Archives: pp. 20, 23, 25, 30, 35, 37, 39, 42, 44, 46, 47, 49; U. S. Army Photo: pp. 28, 58; The Bettmann Archive: pp. 52, 56.

Library of Congress Cataloging-in-Publication Data

McGowen, Tom.
    Go for Broke : Japanese Americans in World War II / Tom McGowen.
        p. cm. — (A First book)
    Includes bibliographical references and index.
    ISBN 0-531-20195-3 (lib. bdg.)
    1. World War, 1939–1945—Japanese Americans. 2. World War, 1939–
    1945—Campaigns. 3. Japanese Americans—History—20th century.
    I. Title. II. Series.
D753.8.M34 1995
940.54'04—dc20   94-39906
                                                                    CIP
                                                                    AC

CONTENTS

AMERICANS IN CONCENTRATION CAMPS

$\mathcal{A}$s the year 1941 drew to a close, every major nation in the world except the United States was in the grip of World War II. In Europe, the armies of Nazi Germany had conquered Poland, France, Belgium, Holland, Denmark, Norway, Yugoslavia, and Greece and had pushed deep into Russia. In North Africa, the forces of the British Empire were engaged in a fierce struggle with the Germans and their Italian allies. In Asia, the armies of the empire of Japan, an ally of Germany and Italy, had conquered part of China and were pushing further into the country.

America had declared itself neutral, but most Americans knew it would not be much longer before the United States became involved in the warfare. The country had been preparing for some time. In 1940, a draft law had

Smoke pours from the crippled U.S. battleships *Tennessee* and *West Virginia*, following the Japanese empire's air attack on Pearl Harbor.

been passed, making every man of a certain age and in good health eligible to be picked to serve in the army. Hundreds of thousands had already been called. A number of automobile factories had retooled and were beginning to produce tanks and military vehicles for the war. Aircraft manufacturers were turning out warplanes. As the last month of 1941 began, Americans went about their daily lives hoping the nation could stay out of the war for a while yet.

But the blow fell suddenly. On December 7, without declaring war first, planes of the Japanese navy launched an air attack on the U.S. naval base at Pearl Harbor, Hawaii, where most of the U.S. Pacific Fleet lay peacefully at anchor. Caught by surprise, three main battleships were sunk, a dozen others were heavily damaged, many planes were destroyed, and thousands of men were killed and injured. Within a week, the United States was officially at war with Japan, Germany, and Italy.

At the time of the Pearl Harbor attack there were about 127,000 people of Japanese descent living in the United States, mostly on the West Coast. About 47,000 were people who had come to America from Japan, and who, because of a discriminatory law that existed then, could not become U.S. citizens. (Until 1943, no Asians were permitted to apply for citizenship.) But the other 80,000 or so were young men and women who had been born in the United States and were therefore, according to the U.S. Constitution, American citizens and entitled to all the same rights, freedoms, and protections that all other citizens had. Among Japanese-Americans they were known as *Nisei* (nee-SAY), which means "second generation" in Japanese.

Most of the *Nisei* were in their late teens or early twenties in 1941. Aside from their differences in appearance, these young Japanese-Americans were just like young Irish Americans, Polish Americans, Italian Americans, and all the other young people of various ethnic groups. They ate hamburgers and drank Cokes, jitterbugged (a popular dance among young Americans at that time), and listened to the records of Glenn Miller and Artie Shaw, just as all the other young people did. Like other young male Americans, *Nisei* men had to register for the draft, and many of them were in the army at the time of the attack on Pearl Harbor. When America went to war, most *Nisei* men wanted to fight to defend their country just as most other young American men did.

But something that many Japanese-Americans had been worried about now happened. The Japanese immigrants and their children had often been subjected to a great deal of racial intolerance and dislike from many of their neighbors on the West Coast. They had often feared that if war ever broke out between Japan and the United States, they would be treated as enemies. And that was exactly what took place. Following the attack on Pearl Harbor there was, naturally, a wave of anger and hatred against the Japanese empire throughout the United States. Tragically, this hatred and anger was also directed against Japanese-Americans. As far as many people were concerned, all Japanese were alike; all Japanese were enemies, whether they had been born in America or not.

Young Japanese Americans, such as these shown enlisting in the army, were as eager to fight for their country as all other young Americans were.

People of Japanese ancestry were not liked and
not wanted on the West Coast in the 1930s.

There was a feeling that Japanese-Americans could not
be trusted, that they were loyal to Japan rather than the
United States. There were rumors that many of them

were actually spies. In his newspaper column, a popular right-wing columnist wrote, "The Japanese in California should be under guard, to the last man and woman."

So, Japanese-Americans suddenly found themselves under suspicion. When young *Nisei* men tried to enlist in the army, as did many thousands of young men after the Pearl Harbor attack, they were turned away. Many *Nisei* who were already in the army were literally kicked out. And after a time, all *Nisei* were even removed from the draft—they would no longer be considered for service in the U.S. Armed Forces.

Things quickly got worse for Japanese-Americans. Military leaders were concerned about the possibility that Japanese-Americans might commit acts of sabotage against army and navy bases, bridges, docks, and rail-roads on the West Coast. On February 19, 1942, the U.S. secretary of war (now known as the secretary of defense) was given the authority to order the removal of people from areas that were important to national defense. It was obvious to Japanese-Americans that *they* were the ones who were going to be removed. For a while, Japanese-Americans who lived in such areas were allowed to leave on their own, and some simply packed up and moved to cities far in the East, such as Chicago and Philadelphia. But then, throughout April and May 1941, thousands of Japanese-Americans on the West Coast were given a week to get ready. Then, under guard by soldiers, they were loaded onto buses and taken to specially built "assembly centers." These were actually nothing less than concentration camps. They consisted

Posters (above) informed Japanese Americans they must move into relocation camps. (left) A mother and children wait to be taken to a camp.

of rows of long wooden buildings, like army barracks, surrounded by barbed-wire fences and overlooked by guard
towers at which armed soldiers stood watch. Thus, one
day all these Japanese-Americans were free citizens, with
their own homes and businesses, and the next day they
were prisoners of concentration camps. It is a sad fact
that almost no other Americans protested against this
absolutely unlawful violation of the constitutional rights
of Japanese-American citizens. Most other Americans
seemed to feel that because the federal government was
doing it, it must be right. Only a few *Nisei* continued after
the internment to fight through the courts for the constitutional rights they knew were theirs.

This was not only a frightening experience for
Japanese-Americans, it was also a bitter and humiliating
one, for most of them were loyal Americans who loved
their country. And for *Nisei* men it was particularly painful.
They wanted to fight for their country, to prove their loyalty, but they weren't going to be allowed to!

**U.S. Navy sailors guard a Japanese-
American restaurant, whose owner
had been relocated, to protect it from
vandalism and looting.**

"REMEMBER PEARL HARBOR" AND "GO FOR BROKE"

The Japanese-Americans did not stay in the "assembly centers." By November 1942, all of them had been moved into permanent camps called "wartime communities." But these "communities" were all located in remote, mostly desert areas, and they, too, were surrounded with barbed-wire fences and patrolled by armed soldiers. They were still nothing more than concentration camps.

But while thousands of Japanese-Americans were trying to get used to living in shacklike rooms and standing in line for meals, a number of government officials in Washington were beginning to argue that *Nisei* should be allowed to fight for their country as many had said they wanted to. The main reason for this was that the propaganda experts of the Japanese empire were trying to convince people of the Asian countries they had conquered, that America was fighting a racist, anti-Asiatic war against *them*. The Japanese were pointing out to Filipinos, Indonesians, and others that they and the Japanese were all Asian and should stand together against the racist Americans. American leaders were counting on help from these people against the Japanese and felt they had to counter the Japanese propaganda. What better way to show that America was not anti-Asian than by having men of Asian ancestry in the United States Armed Forces? By the end of January 1943, government and military leaders had agreed to create an all-*Nisei* "showpiece" military unit.

Actually, there already *was* an all-*Nisei* unit in the U.S. Army. The Hawaiian National Guard, which was made up mostly of Japanese-Americans (Hawaii had a Japanese-American population of about 160,000), had been made part of the U.S. Army in 1941. In June 1942, when Japanese-Americans in the United States were being put into concentration camps, the Hawaiian *Nisei* soldiers, 1,404 strong, had their weapons taken away from them, were put onto a troopship, and taken to California. From there, they were whisked across the country by train to Camp McCoy, Wisconsin. They were officially designated the 100th Infantry Battalion and spent their time training with wooden dummy rifles. All the while, the army tried to decide what to do with them. Many top army officers did not trust the *Nisei* and were reluctant to let them have real weapons.

Aware of this, the men of the 100th Infantry Battalion

Most internment camps for Japanese Americans were rows of identical wooden houses in a bleak, windswept desert setting such as this.

believed they would never be permitted to go into combat. They expected to be used as a general work unit, unloading supplies, cleaning up military bases, and so on. This hurt and angered them, for they desperately wanted to fight for their country to prove their loyalty. Soon after the plan for an all-*Nisei* unit was approved in Washington, however, they were told they were going to be formed into a combat unit. Many of the men were so overjoyed that they actually jumped up and down and cheered. Shortly, they were sent to Camp Shelby, Mississippi, for final training.

It was customary for newly formed military units to select a motto; the *Nisei* of the 100th Infantry Battalion chose as their motto the phrase "Remember Pearl Harbor." This was a slogan that was widespread throughout the United States. It appeared on signs fastened on the walls of just about every restaurant and tavern in the country, it was regularly printed on the front page of many newspapers, and it was even the title of a popular song that was played on radio programs many times a day in the early months of the war. For Americans, the Japanese surprise attack on Pearl Harbor had been a low, sneaky, treacherous act, and what "Remember Pearl Harbor" meant to Americans was, "Don't forget what the Japanese did at Pearl Harbor and let's make them pay for it!"

Meanwhile, the army was gathering other *Nisei* together. There was a number of Japanese-Americans who had been allowed to stay in the army when most others had been forced to leave, and they now received orders to report to Camp Shelby. The army asked for vol-

Finally allowed to serve their country, *Nisei* soldiers of the U.S. Army arrive at their training center, Camp Shelby, Mississippi.

A typical poster of World War II urges Americans to remember Pearl Harbor. *Nisei* soldiers of the 100th Infantry Battalion took this as their motto.

unteers from the Japanese-Americans of Hawaii and got more than 10,000, of whom they took 2,686. These men, too, were sent to Camp Shelby.

The army also sent recruiters into the concentration camps. After the shabby treatment they had been given and after seeing their rights as citizens simply ignored, many of the *Nisei* were no longer willing to fight for a country that had done such things to them. But about 2,500 men did volunteer; of these, about 1,500 were accepted and sent to Camp Shelby.

All the men were organized into what the army called a regimental combat team. About 3,300 of them were formed into the 442nd Infantry Regiment, consisting of three units, called battalions, of about 870 riflemen each, plus a cannon company, an antitank company, and a service company (trucks and Jeeps for carrying troops and supplies). The other men were formed into the 522nd Artillery Battalion (armed with sixteen large cannons), the 232nd Combat Engineer Company (men specially trained to quickly put bridges across rivers, and so on), and a service unit. The entire group was officially designated the 442nd Regimental Combat Team. At first, with the exception of Captain Pershing Nakada, who commanded the combat engineers company, none of the officers were Japanese-Americans.

For their motto, the men of the 442nd picked the phrase "Go for Broke." This was a Hawaiian slang term used by players of the dice game "craps," and it meant "to risk everything on one roll of the dice." For the *Nisei*

Nisei soldiers of the 442nd Regiment undergoing special training. Japanese-American soldiers were noted for training particularly hard.

of the 442nd it meant, "Give everything you have—give your *all*!"

In training, the *Nisei* showed exactly what their motto meant to them. They did everything faster, harder, and better than most of the other troops in training. They set a new camp record for making a 25-mile (40-km) march with full packs on, doing it in a much faster time than any other unit had ever done it. In a kind of war game that was set up to check the abilities of the troops in training—involving many different army units on two opposing sides—the umpires ruled that the 442nd "destroyed" most of a force that outnumbered them three to one. It was obvious that the 442nd was turning into what the army called an "elite" unit—soldiers of the very highest quality!

3 MAKING A NAME IN ITALY

The first of the two all-*Nisei* units to get into the war was the 100th Infantry Battalion. In August 1943, it was shipped to North Africa. The Allies (Americans, British, and French) had defeated the German and Italian forces there and were now putting together armies for an invasion of Italy.

At first, it seemed as if no one wanted the 100th Infantry Battalion. Many high-ranking army officers simply did not believe that these men of Asian ancestry, many of whom were not much more than 5 feet (1.5 m) tall, could be good fighters. Gen. Mark Clark, commander of the army the 100th would be part of, planned to use them as nothing more than guards for railroad yards and supply depots. But the 100th's commanding officer, Col. Farrant Turner, persuaded Clark and others that the *Nisei*

Lt. Gen. Mark Clark, commander of the U.S. 5th
Army said of the Japanese-American troops,
"I've never had such fine soldiers!"

could fight well if they were given a chance. Finally, it was agreed to let them become part of the 133rd Infantry Regiment, replacing a battalion that had been taken from the regiment for special duty. The 133rd Regiment was part of the 34th Division of the Fifth Army. (A division was formed of three infantry regiments plus artillery, engineers, and service troops.) The *Nisei* were gratified to find that the soldiers of the 133rd Regiment accepted them as comrades without hesitation.

When the Fifth Army invaded Italy on September 9, the 34th Division was kept behind as a "reserve" unit, to be called if needed. Things quickly began to go wrong for the invasion, and the 34th was soon needed. On September 19, it landed in Italy and hurried forward to join the American forces already locked in battle with the tough, experienced German army. The Germans were determined to make the Americans pay in blood for every foot of ground they moved across.

On the morning of September 29, the 100th Infantry Battalion had its first encounter with the German army. The 100th was moving up a road at the head of the 133rd Regiment when machine-gun fire slashed through the air. A squad (twelve men) of *Nisei* commanded by Sgt. Shigeo Takata, moved forward to take out the hidden machine-gun nest. They did so, but then German artillery shells began landing in the area, and Sergeant Takata was killed: the first man of the 100th to be killed in action. In the afternoon, the 100th made an attack on a strongly defended German position, driving the German soldiers into retreat and destroying a tank. By the end of its first

General Clark inspects a much-decorated unit, the all Japanese-American 100th Infantry Battalion.

day in combat, the 100ᵗʰ had lost one man, sixteen were wounded, and two of its men had been named to receive medals for bravery. It had defeated all the enemy soldiers it had gone up against. Within a week, General Clark had informed his superior, "I've never had such fine soldiers. Send me all you've got!" The fighting ability of Japanese-American soldiers was never again questioned.

The Germans pulled back into the rugged mountains of southern Italy. In front of these mountains flowed the Volturno River. On the night of October 12–13, the 133ʳᵈ Regiment, with the 100ᵗʰ Battalion again at the front, crossed the river and found the Germans awaiting them. Within an area extending some 30 to 40 miles (48 to 64 km) behind the river, the Germans had prepared three lines of defense, each stronger than the one before it. These lines consisted of strings of fortified cannon and machine-gun emplacements with tangles of barbed-wire and explosive mines that would go off if stepped on. The *Nisei* battalion and the rest of the regiment began fighting their way through these obstacles. Often moving through downpours of rain, driving sleet, and fogs that shrouded the mountains, they were raked with machine-gun fire and hammered with artillery fire. It took more than two weeks to get through the German's first line, and it was well into January 1944 before the third line was even reached.

Another river, the Rapido, wound in front of the third line. The Germans had caused it to flood for a number of miles by opening dams, so that the ground on the American side was a watery marsh, almost impossible

Army engineers disarm
explosive devices
planted by the Germans
to prevent the advance
of U.S. troops.
Stepping on these
meant injury or death!

for men or vehicles to get through. It was also mined, with the kind of mines that would jump a few feet into the air when stepped on and explode, with a whirling cluster of jagged metal pieces ripping into a man's chest or stomach. A path had to be cleared through the mines, the river had to be crossed, and then, on the other side— more mines, and open ground that would be seared by machine-gun and artillery fire!

The first attempt to cross the river, by the U.S. 36th Division, was a horrible, bloody failure. On January 24, it was the 34th Division's turn to try, with the 133rd Regiment leading the way. Exploding mines and German artillery drove them back. More attempts were made, but it was a week before the three battalions of the 133rd Regiment managed to get across the river and stay there—and their casualties were terrible.

Once across, the three battalions fanned out. While one began the slow, deadly job of fighting its way through a small city by the river, the other battalion and the 100th Infantry Battalion charged up into the hills. Almost at once, the *Nisei* found themselves pinned down by a deadly attack of German tanks. Pvt. Masao Awakuni took on the tanks with a bazooka (a weapon that fires rocket missiles) and destroyed one, causing the others to withdraw. The *Nisei* then cleared all German troops off the hill.

But now, German resistance stiffened. The 34th Division was across the river, but it could not advance any further. It was under constant artillery fire and frequent fierce attacks by German infantry. In addition, because of the cold, wet conditions, many men were suffering from

Pvt. First Class Masao Awakuni of the
100th Infantry Battalion, who single-
handedly destroyed a German tank

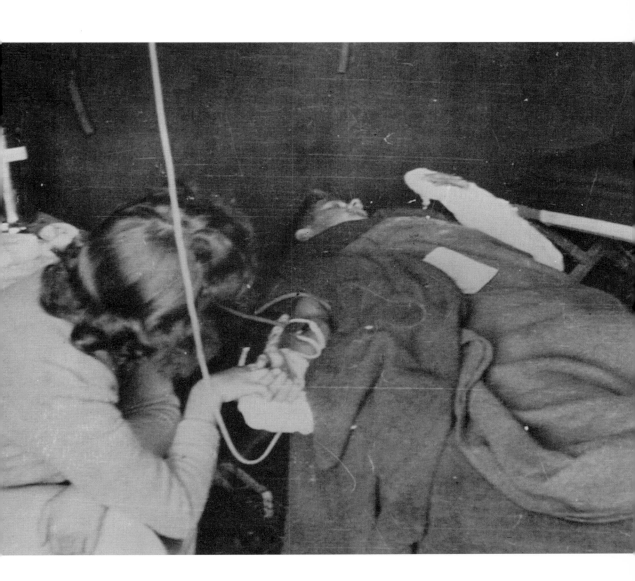

Nisei troops suffered enormous casualties. This man, wounded by a bullet, receives a blood transfusion administered by an army nurse.

trench foot, a crippling affliction similar to frostbite, and many were ill with influenza and pneumonia.

And by now, the casualties were appalling. Of the fourteen hundred men of the 100th Infantry Battalion that had originally come from Hawaii, some nine hundred had been killed or wounded since landing in Italy. The whole 34th Division had been so bloodied by the Rapido crossing and the battles on the other side that on February 14 it was taken out of the combat area for a rest. To replace the soldiers lost to the 100th Battalion, men from the First Battalion of the 442nd *Nisei* Regiment, which was still training in America, were sent to join the 100th, so that it could continue to be an all-*Nisei* fighting unit.

The 100th's "rest" turned out to be a short one. Allied forces had made a surprise landing further up the coast of Italy in an attempt to get behind the German's third line of defense. But they had run into serious trouble, and in March the 34th Division, as well as the 100th Infantry Battalion, was sent to help.

The Allied force that made the landing had been able to capture only a small section of beach. It had fought off German attacks that tried to push it back into the sea but remained pinned down and unable to advance. Now, reinforced by the 34th and other divisions, the Allies were able to slowly push forward. During April and May, the 100th Infantry Battalion was in the forefront of this advance.

By June 2, the German's third line of defense had finally been broken, and the Allies were advancing everywhere. On this day, the 442nd Regimental Combat Team arrived in Italy to begin its part in the war. It arrived with

Following retreating German forces, men of the 100th Infantry Battalion slog along a dusty road in Italy.

only two infantry battalions, because virtually all the men of its First Battalion had been sent to Italy already to replace the men lost to the 100th Infantry Battalion. Therefore, the 100th now became the first battalion of the 442nd. Eighty-four hundred strong, the *Nisei* were ready to take on the enemy.

The Germans were in retreat, but they were far from beaten. They formed a new line of defense north of Rome, and on June 26, the 442nd fought its first battle against those defenses, near the little town of Suvoreto. Once more the Germans pulled back, fighting delaying battles. The *Nisei* were involved in most of these, at the towns of Luviana and Leghorn, and at Belvedere where they encountered a battalion of one of the German Army's best units—the Hermann Goering division—and beat it. Moving through these towns in pursuit of the Germans, the *Nisei* and other Americans learned to be careful about picking things up or touching things, for the Germans left thousands of "booby traps." A candy bar, a bar of soap, or even a pencil might explode and kill or injure a soldier if picked up. Sitting in a chair, opening a window, or flushing a toilet might trigger a deadly explosion.

In August, the Germans created a new defensive line across the Arno River, in northern Italy. The 442nd was one of the units that crossed the Arno, pushing the Germans back again. The Germans had been astonished at the sight of all these obviously Asian men in American uniforms. Some of those taken prisoner asked if Japan had renounced its alliance with Germany and taken sides

A gun crew of the 552nd Artillery Battalion keeps up a steady barrage of fire against retreating German troops.

with America. By now, the *Nisei* had gained a reputation in the Fifth Army as a tough, hard-hitting, dependable fighting unit—one of the best. It was known that they fought with tremendous courage, and their casualties were substantial.

Back home, these men's fathers and mothers, sisters and brothers, wives and girlfriends, were still prisoners in concentration camps.

A RESCUE
AND A
BREAKTHROUGH

In September, the 442nd was taken out of Italy and sent into southern France, where, as in Italy, Allied forces were striving to push the Germans out of strong defensive positions in rugged mountains. Here, the *Nisei* were made part of the U.S. 36th Division of the Seventh Army.

The *Nisei* were put into action in mid-October and immediately found themselves in a bitter fight to capture a town called Bruyeres. The Germans held the town and the area in front of it, and the *Nisei* had to fight their way through machine-gun nests into the town, then fight from house to house, against men firing from upper windows and machines guns firing from basements. By the end of the day, the 442nd had killed and captured more than two hundred Germans, and the town was theirs.

Moving out! Soldiers of the 442nd Regimental Combat Team pile into a truck headed for a combat area in France.

Because of their reputation as a hard-fighting unit that could be depended on, the *Nisei* were picked for a special mission—the rescue of a trapped American battalion. The First Battalion of the 36th Division's 141st Infantry Regiment had been sent to capture a ridge held by the Germans. But the battalion had been surrounded and was now pinned down under enemy fire. Its soldiers were running short of water and many were seriously wounded. The *Nisei* were assigned to try to break through the German forces surrounding the battalion and help it withdraw to safety.

The three battalions of the 442nd moved forward in line, making their way through the heavily forested mountain region. They were soon spotted, and German artillery began firing on them. The shells hit trees and exploded, sending whirlwinds of shattered branches, wooden splinters, and metal fragments among the Japanese-American soldiers. Many men began to drop, but the *Nisei* grimly pushed on. They were going "for broke!"

They began to encounter groups of German infantry, dug in and determined to stop them. The *Nisei* cleared them out of the way with headlong charges in which they used hand grenades and bayonets. For three days, with steadily rising casualties, they moved on until they reached the trapped battalion, which was now down to only 211 men.

The *Nisei*, however, were not finished with their job. They pushed on and captured the ridge that the trapped battalion had been unable to take. Then they continued down the slope of the hill into the valley below. By doing

The best time of day! Soldiers of the
442nd move along the chow line in
an encampment in France.

this, they split the German forces apart so that the whole 36th Division was able to come pouring in between them. By November 15, the Germans were in full retreat.

But the 442nd had suffered brutal casualties. Since coming to France it had lost 140 men and 674 had been wounded—nearly the strength of a whole battalion. And, as in Italy, many of the uninjured men were crippled with trench foot or ill with influenza or pneumonia. Accordingly, the 442nd was taken out of combat for a rest. Its losses were replaced by *Nisei* volunteers from Hawaii and the United States.

Many U.S. government officials were now aware of the achievements of the 442nd, and their minds changed about Japanese-Americans. Some were arguing that the American concentration camps should be closed. On December 18, 1944, the U.S. Supreme Court unanimously ruled that all Japanese-Americans in concentration camps had to be freed. Of course, this was joyful news for the *Nisei* soldiers in Europe.

In spring 1945, the 442nd was sent back to Italy, where the Allies were about to assault the final defensive line the Germans had formed in the northeastern mountains. The 442nd was made one of the three regiments of the U.S. 92nd Infantry Division, which also included the all-African American 370th Infantry, and the all-white American 473rd Infantry.

The presence of the 442nd was carefully kept secret so that the Germans wouldn't know this hard-fighting unit was back in Italy. The Fifth Army intended to use the *Nisei* for another special mission. They were going to lead

The color guard (flag guard) of the 442nd stands in a
position of honor during a ceremony honoring their
comrades who received medals for bravery.

**Artillerymen of the 552nd Artillery Battalion
prepare a cannon shell for firing.**

the 92nd Division in an attack on the best-defended part of the German line. But the attack would actually be a "diversion"—intended to make the Germans think it was the main thing and draw their attention away from where the real attack would take place.

The German positions were on the peaks of jagged mountains that overlooked the whole Italian coastline. On the night of April 4, the *Nisei* of the Third Battalion began an eight-hour climb in darkness up the side of a mountain on which the slightest misstep might send a man tumbling 100 feet (30 km) or more. Reaching the top, they fanned out and struck, catching the Germans by surprise. Using tommy guns (automatic weapons) and hand grenades in a series of bloody face-to-face fights, they drove the Germans out of their positions and sent them fleeing. Meanwhile, the 100th Battalion had attacked a peak to the north and, after twenty minutes of bitter fighting, gained its objective. On still another mountaintop, the Second Battalion was also wiping out its opposition.

All three battalions continued to push on, with the other regiments of the division providing whatever help they could. By April 8, the 442nd's Third Battalion had reached a vital highway and gained control of it. The "diversion" had now turned into a full breakthrough along the west coast of Italy. On April 15, the entire Fifth Army launched the main attack and the Germans were finished. They had fought hard and skillfully for months, but now their line had been broken by the 442nd, and the Fifth Army was cutting them to pieces. By May 2, the war was over in Italy.

The 442nd Regimental Combat Team had one of the highest casualty rates of any U.S. Army unit of World War II—600 dead and 8,886 wounded. This was more than three times the number of men it had started out with! The 442nd was probably the most decorated unit in the

At a memorial service in Italy, Japanese-American soldiers bow their heads in respect for comrades who lost their lives in combat.

army. Its men were awarded more than eighteen thousand medals for bravery, and the entire unit won forty-three division commendations, thirteen army commendations, two meritorious service unit plaques, and *seven* presidential distinguished unit citations—the very highest award that can be given by the United States to an entire military unit.

5 JAPANESE-AMERICANS VERSUS THE JAPANESE EMPIRE

Slowly and cautiously, trying not to make the slightest noise, Roy Matsumoto squirmed through the thick underbrush of a jungle in Burma. Somewhere ahead of him, he knew, was a group of Japanese soldiers, and he hoped to get close enough to hear what they were talking about. He would be able to understand them, for he spoke Japanese perfectly. But if they discovered him, he was a dead man! They wouldn't just take him prisoner, they would shoot him, or even torture him, for being a spy and traitor—because he looked like them.

After what seemed an eternity of crawling, he heard voices. Lying still and straining to listen, Roy overheard the soldiers discussing an attack they were about to make. It would be an attack on the American unit to

Japanese-American translators often accompanied troops into combat on the islands in the Pacific theater of the war.

which Roy belonged! Carefully, he wriggled himself around and began to crawl back to report what he had heard. Thus, when the Japanese made their attack, the Americans were ready for them with an ambush. The attackers were wiped out, and Roy Matsumoto was later awarded the Legion of Merit medal for his bravery in risking his life to crawl out and learn the enemy's plans.

Roy Matsumoto was one of many *Nisei* who, long before the 442nd Regimental Combat Team began making a name for itself in Europe, were doing a magnificent job of helping to defeat the Japanese empire in the Pacific war zone. After the war was over, U.S. military leaders agreed that what these Japanese-Americans did probably helped shorten the war in the Pacific by a good two years and saved at least a million Americans lives! The *Nisei* in the Pacific region were a "secret weapon" that provided American commanders with information that was tremendously useful in planning attacks on or defenses against the Japanese.

How this was done was with *language*. The Japanese language is extremely complicated and hard for foreigners to learn. Because of this, Japanese army and navy officers believed their language was actually an unbreakable code. They felt quite safe writing orders, marking maps, and sending radio messages in plain Japanese. They never knew that all through the war many of these orders and messages were being seen or heard by Japanese-Americans who understood them perfectly well and passed on vital information to American commanders.

The *Nisei* doing this important work were men who had volunteered, some even before the war began, to become part of a Japanese-speaking army intelligence (information-gathering) unit. They had gone to a special secret school to polish up their knowledge of Japanese, then had been sent to places in the Pacific war zone where they could be most useful. Many of them were put with combat troops, where fighting was going on. These men skillfully questioned captured Japanese soldiers and read captured documents—orders, diaries, letters, and so on. This work often provided a great deal of useful data about Japanese troop locations and movements, supplies, fortifications, and battle plans.

At first, most of the top American generals and admirals didn't think the work of the Japanese-American translators would be of much use. But something happened that changed that very suddenly. In 1942, on the island of Guadalcanal, where American and Japanese battled for months, a thick booklet, written in Japanese, was found by some Americans. The book was taken to the team of three *Nisei* translators working on the island. They quickly discovered that the book was an official manual of the Japanese navy, containing a list of all of Japan's warships, their code names, their speed and weapons, the bases they were stationed at—information that not even the cleverest spy could have obtained! This was of tremendous value to the top commanders of the U.S. Navy in planning operations against the Japanese. The call quickly went out to send more *Nisei* translators to the Pacific!

The work of these translators was not at all safe nor

Nisei **student translators learning their craft at the Military Intelligence Service Language School at Fort Snelling.**

U.S. Marines stormed onto the Japanese-held island of Guadalcanal in 1942. *Nisei* translators did extremely important work there.

danger-free. The *Nisei* were often under fire and at as much risk as any of the combat soldiers they were with. They were close to the enemy and in danger of being captured, which could mean torture and death for them. They were even in danger from their own side, because American soldiers, seeing their Asian faces, might think they were enemies and shoot them. Some *Nisei* were killed and wounded by just such tragic mistakes.

The translators sometimes deliberately put themselves in even greater danger. On islands that had been captured by American troops, groups of Japanese soldiers would often "hole up" in a cave, determined to fight to the death rather than surrender. Of course, this could mean the deaths of many more American soldiers. So, Japanese-speaking *Nisei* would try to talk the Japanese soldiers out of their plan and get them to give up. But while they were talking, the *Nisei* risked being shot by fanatical enemy soldiers. Like Roy Matsumoto, a large number of *Nisei* translators were awarded medals for bravery in risking their lives in many ways.

There were also a number of *Nisei* who were not translators or who were not in the 442nd Regimental Combat Team nor the 100th Infantry Battalion—but who played parts in the war. One was an infantryman with one of the divisions that made the invasion of North Africa in 1942; he rose to the rank of colonel by the war's end. Another was an aerial gunner who flew on fifty-eight bombing missions and was awarded the Distinguished Flying Cross and the Air Medal. And there were others. According to the records, 33,300 *Nisei*, some of them

American soldiers blow up a dugout of Japanese soldiers determined to fight to the death, despite a *Nisei* translator's efforts to make them surrender.

women, served in the U.S. armed forces during World War II. Despite the suspicion, intolerance, and outright hatred they had been subjected to by some other Americans, and despite the terrible injustice many of them had suffered by being forced into concentration camps, these Americans of Japanese ancestry served their country and proved themselves many times over. Today, Japanese-Americans, like all Americans, should be respected for their contributions to the military efforts of World War II and for the positive contributions their children and grandchildren have made throughout the country.

FOR
FURTHER
READING

Katz, William Loren. *World War II to the New Frontier, 1940–1963*. Austin, Tex.: Raintree Steck-Vaughn, 1993.

Kitano, Harry. *Japanese Americans, Racism and Renewal*. New York: Orchard Books, 1990.

Leathers, Noel L. *The Japanese in America*. Minneapolis: Lerner, 1991.

Stein, R. Conrad. *Nisei Regiment*. Chicago: Childrens Press, 1985.

Wright, David K. *A Multicultural Portrait of World War II*. New York: Marshall Cavendish, 1994.

INDEX

ABOUT THE AUTHOR

Tom McGowen was born in 1927, grew up with an intense interest in military history, and eventually served in the U.S. Navy in World War II. In his war books for juvenile readers, he says he attempts to help readers understand that battles and campaigns were fought for a specific purpose, or strategy, and did not simply "happen."

Mr. McGowen, who lives in Norridge, Illinois, is the author of more than forty books, including thirteen written for Franklin Watts. His most recent Franklin Watts First Book was *Lonely Eagles and Buffalo Soldiers: African Americans in World War II*. In 1986, his book *Radioactivity: From the Curies to the Atomic Age* (Franklin Watts) was named an NSTA-CBC Outstanding Science Trade Book for Children. Mr. McGowen also won the 1990 Children's Reading Roundtable Award for Outstanding Contribution to the Field of Juvenile Literature.